THE GLASS SWARM

THE GLASS SWARM

Peter Bennet

FlambardPress

First published in Great Britain in 2008 by Flambard Press
Stable Cottage, East Fourstones, Hexham NE47 5DX
www.flambardpress.co.uk

Typeset by BookType
Cover Design by Gainford Design Associates
Printed in Great Britain by Cromwell Press, Trowbridge, Wiltshire

A CIP catalogue record for this book
is available from the British Library.
ISBN: 978-1-873226-99-5

Flambard Press wishes to thank Arts Council England
for its financial support.

Flambard Press is a member of Inpress

Mixed Sources
Product group from well-managed
forests and other controlled sources
www.fsc.org Cert no. TT-COC-2082
© 1996 Forest Stewardship Council
FSC

For Sue, who listens to them all, with love

Acknowledgements

Poems in this collection have appeared in the following anthologies: *Both Sides of Hadrian's Wall* from Selkirk Lapwing Press, *North by North East* from Iron Press, *Speaking English*, a festschrift for John Lucas, from Five Leaves Press, and *Still Standen*, a festschrift for Michael Standen, from Other Poetry Editions. Thanks are due to the editors: Robert Leach, Andy Croft, Cynthia Fuller, and James Roderick Burns. 'The Redesdale Rowan' was commissioned by Culture North East for the Sense of Place project. 'Snow in Northumberland: An Effusion' was commissioned by New Writing North and Arts Council England and published on www.acknowledgedland.com.

Contents

I only know that there was something more than I have written that alarmed me, but whether it was sound or sight I am not able to remember.

M.R. James, 'Count Magnus'

SIR ENTREPRENEUR

Between the workers and the wealth is strife
in regions perilous to honest men,
where goblins chuckle and the marsh fire burns.
Your brave steed trembles, and his eyes roll madly.

Put up your visor, and let me escort
you onward safely, for the light grows dim
and soon the path breaks, as it drops
in zigzags through enchanted hangers

where roots rear up and watchful stones
lie bedded under quilts of moss.
We shall discover, while the day still lingers,
an elfin briefcase in the queachy ferns

and in it costings you have need of badly
to smooth the feathers of your auditors,
the ravens and the hooded crows.
You'll be their breakfast if you show a loss.

Those creaks we hear are limb on limb
as dead trees clutch their living kin,
like bankrupts and their creditors
pulled down by ivy on the muddy slopes.

Your shield is smirched. Your plume hangs sadly.
Lord may I say, with your permission,
my castle stands a bow-shot hence.
Five hundred businessmen are there, each one

at wine beside his lady wife
in merry conclave and good countenance,
and if your errand may be deemed the sort
to turn a profit, they will fund you gladly.

THE NATURALIST

The Reverend Collingwood Pringle writes to his son, 1862

Inland we have another burning day,
but you, I trust, are cooler by the sea
in that calm haven out of reach,
while your fine fads and theories bedevil
the task of men who preach revealed religion.
Wild roses are now done but here and there
a field of uncut grass contains
spikes of sorrel standing to attention
among the moon-faced dog-daisies
you call *chrysanthemum leucanthemums*.
Beside our stream, the green-scaled dragonflies
are plentiful and heavy on the air,
with small ones too, you will remember,
like fragile tubes of blue, winged glass.
You see, I'm quite the naturalist.

I wonder if, when one decides to free
oneself from something – duty, or a place –
you've noticed that a pause occurs
sufficient to allow the future
to squeeze into a smaller space?
Sometimes, I think, such pauses last forever.
I'm sleepy and imagine only
the dull façade of that hotel – your face
inclined towards your specimens
and notebooks, on a balcony
reflected by a sea-slicked beach
the bogus progress of the waves leaves level –
and every day no letter comes.
Meanwhile, this five-pound note and scribble travel
with love from one no longer young or clever.

THE PRIVATE VIEW

As if in a film by Eric Rohmer

Within the Musée d'Art Contemporain,
vast canvases of his, with pigment-clumps
like brains of cabbage roses in a fog,

are upstaged by the barefaced *chic*
with which she slides her hand inside his shirt.
There is a source of daylight, well concealed,

high in the ceiling of the atrium,
to which his longing to be reconciled
with spontaneity and mischief jumps

and joins the dust's unending jitterbug.
I think he'll take her home with him, but then
adjust the tempo to the speed of art

and make her sleep alone on his divan,
yet let her ticket for the Paris train
remain for years between the sleek

unhelpful pages of the catalogue
to leave, in time, a faint pink stain
like lipstick when she next day pecks his cheek.

THE SILVER OF THE MIRROR

*'In time his expences brought clamours about him, that
overpowered the lamb's bleat and the linnet's song; and the
groves were haunted by beings very different from fawns
and fairies.'*
    Samuel Johnson, *The Life of Shenstone*

As if reflected by the street, the soil
he stands on, with his long nose raised
to sniff the nearness of the revolution,
accepts the clean blade of his hoe
and scatters slowly, as through antique glass.
It is a matter of above, below.
He wears knee-breeches and a tricorn hat,
and mumbles verse into his plain jabot
of which he is the pleased but modest author.
His mild voice coaxes lawns and trees
to ripple through translucent tarmac,
still carrying the sentiments
he adds to them, on painted plaques,
of Thoughtfulness, of Sadness, and of Pity.
We tear the pavements up to reach his garden
and roar like beasts in pain, as boundaries break
to find ourselves reduced by what we spoil.

And yet we are his comrades, and our horror
an upside-down ideal while, hoof to toe,
we struggle to assist him as we churn
parterres to mud and trample flat
the topiary and pergolas
he has maintained are beautiful, and wreck
the patterned walks, the symmetries
he laid out to reflect unchanging order.
The dream is his, and ours the revelation
that animates all malcontents.

The rumpus of our anguish fills the city.
Meanwhile, within the silver of the mirror,
beyond the ruined portico
and fountains with their splendours mired to wallow,
the cornfields and the hills where flocks are grazed
are as his verses promise, yet more golden,
and at his feet the seeds of terror grow.

THE BRIGANDS

Our actors are maintaining the *sang froid*
on which punctilio depends,
while chinese lanterns spark and jostle
among the olive trees as if to mock
their frocks and uniforms – too warm to wear
on such a night – and ricochet
the glitter of their jewels and decorations.

They have enjoyed the buffet with champagne,
attended by what passes for nobility
in this poor province, and now dance a little –
although the wind is sagging the marquee –
to music from a gipsy trio
before their moonlit progress to the ruins.
I think the steamer has now left the bay.

The air is cooling, and civility
will yield to mayhem as the play begins,
so wake up and uncork another bottle.
Art holds her mirror, but the finest drama
falls flat beside the unaffected antics
of private persons, as they wrestle
with keen and unambiguous emotions.

You will be entertained by what occurs.
This squall will suit the purpose of our brigands
quite perfectly, those murderous romantics
composed of ruthlessness and brio,
recruited by my agent, the *chanteuse*
in smoke-grey chiffon, who presides each summer
at my hotel and makes it pay.

THE SKATER

'This is the first stage of the glaciers generally; it is like bright-plucked water swaying in a pail.'
   Gerard Manley Hopkins, *Journal*

It seems so little time ago: the eyes
of two cigars, and badinage
about the triumph of the master race,
the smell of moonlit ice, your headlong beauty,
and Hopkins at the Grindelwald.
How soon the silliness of silly asses
becomes the moraine of an age!

He grew too careless of his privilege
to reconcile his cause with ours,
or share our vision of the long ascent
to contemplation of the Graal,
and wisdom that allows the bold,
when nothing but the past is present,
to taste the bright-plucked water from the pail.

The inscape flickers, and the damn fool dies
again, while you skate on, your cold
angelic face the moonlight kisses,
serene, as blood spills on the small goatee
he wore in honour of the toiling masses,
and I escape, as is my duty,
by climbing heights our zeal surpasses.

THE SQUIRREL

'Not yet, perhaps not here, but in the end,
And somewhere like this.'
　Philip Larkin

You talk to sunshine on the photograph
that blears our unremembered faces
and mirrors yours within a thin black frame.
Your flowers are very cheerful in their vases.
We did not wish you to be put in here,
or see your footprints as you drag your shins
beneath a floral dressing-gown
across the mop-slicks in the corridor.

Here's where you dream you tripped a snare
that closed forever on a whiff
of disinfectant and a pain that lingers.
You're like the squirrel on the chandelier,
we try to reach you, but our fingers
grasp only air, and up you go,
beyond our help, to where your name
comes vacantly from far below.

You planned to age like poetry:
lyric and elegy becoming one
in celebration of the verb *to be*.
To kiss you, we blot out the sun.
We did not wish you to be made of stuff
morphine can manage till your smile begins
to claim that dying is the same
as painless waking, and no damage done.

QUINCE BLOSSOM

There is no air, each leaf that falls
does so from lassitude, while you push on
through rhododendrons, unkempt quinces.
Why should we mock your axiom
that wishes, forged by settled wills,
are facts that alter circumstances,
or doubt your clever stratagem
to get back somehow to the lawn,
the tilting sundial and the rusty pram,
where lank grass snags your weary toes?
We don't call what you did a sin,
and no one any more knows what you've done
except the two of us, inside your head.
Approach the house. Break down the door.
The only room has furniture
too heavy for the floor, and walls
not quite the colour of your skin:
quince blossom, maybe, or the one
like lamp-light shining through your mother's ear,
as she bends down to kiss your nose
and leave you happy in your little bed
for one last time before she goes.

THE PICKLE TUB

There's still no water in the lake.
And then this morning when the sun
arrived between the shutter bars,
it burned my best arm as I stretched
to let it in but couldn't reach.
I rang, for all the good it did,
and called, but no-one heard me calling.
Poor Daddy had his laces sponged and pressed
each time his shoes were cleaned, his pocket linings
unstitched and laundered every week.
The wood we used to picnic in
when we were girls – and so alike –
that hangs on one side of the hill
above the flooded pumping house,
is now a forest, in which good and evil
giants find and lose each other, brawling.
Go there and join them, I suggest,
and don't come back. I've had enough.
It's obvious that since you died
this pickle tub expands until
tomorrow's bigger, but seems farther off,
and every day speeds up the sense of falling.

DANSE MACABRE

Let's wish the porcelain goodnight, its sleep
unbroken in its cabinet,

and sweet dreams to the Canaletto
of sunlight on a campanile,

obscured by shadows in this swirling room,
adjusting triangles in peace, while steely

ripples widen on smoke-darkened water.
Goodnight to niches in which lilies weep.

Each guest has pleased his opposite:
Uncouthness and Dishevelment

have danced with Ease and Dignity
across the yielding, talc-strewn floor,

Youth has pranced with Age, and Body
has re-engaged with Soul, to tunes

no longer heard, which all the skills
of living orchestras can merely echo.

The black-clad servants are somnambulant.
From off the gallery drop pale balloons

to lift abruptly, as a door
swings open elsewhere, and the draught is sweet.

It's nearly time for rest. The hills
are shedding darkness from their stature

beyond the graveyard, and light saps the gloom
where candles splutter while we sit

in dancing-pumps of dust and draw
cobwebs around us on the window-seat.

CUNEIFORM

These cold walls have been papered with a murder
of crows among grey foliage
but half-obliterated once
in thin emulsion, and the floorboards spattered
as if with guano under dust.
The great desk must have come in through the window
that also lets in moonlight, on a book
forever open, an abandoned page –
the secret of the only code worth cracking –
hand-lettered, as with wedge-shaped splinters.
You would be thrilled to read the curse
in good plain English on the back
that condemns all who meddle in such matters
to be devoured by need to know.

A lidless eye has overlaid the moon.
Be very careful on the creaking
stairs and landing. Where's that ounce
of sense to tell you not to trust
the feeling that, for you, the eye is winking?
When you doss down inside a green cocoon
of sleeping-bag, your tape-recorder
will pick up interrogatory croaking
while still switched off and not in working order.
Outside are prints of crows' feet in the snow
of human size, but you are shrinking
to be pursued through folios of winters
and not wake up to hear the window shattered
or bare your pale skin to an inky beak.

THE REDESDALE ROWAN

From now on I will be dispensing
with ramblers' maps and all desire
to find the flora of this rabbit-lawn
listed in my guidebook to the fells,
or read the secret of the storm-shot rowan –
that should have fallen, yet has berries dancing
blood-red on leafy carousels –
in some botanical grimoire.
The day is warm. My feet are aching.
It is too late, with sunshine in my eyes,
to care which insect air force is commencing
a mass-attack of lullabies.
I shall approach the tree and dream there, waking
to hang my branches with a peal of bells.

THE DEEP SETTEE

The room is empty, but the sun peers in
to where the old springs of the deep
settee twang softly as I pass
right through them – where we sat together –
as if through blown seeds of umbellifers
in settee shape, and chiming tints
of lavender and heliotrope,
that match me, as I swerve and slither,
exactly, in my skin of chintz.
The room is empty but for us
and that pale sunlight, through uncurtained glass,
which, hour by hour, each day delivers
uncertainly, to shrivel up
the little dust heaps where you try to sleep.

THE LENS

Your look is wide-eyed and direct,
while I have puckered eyelids, and my head
between my thumbs to point the lens
and frame your fine-boned fidgeting.
But now it's you that's focused, as you lean
towards the window to inspect
a small boy, busy in the lane,
who is the child we never had
although we prayed each time we fucked.
He has a roving glance, a stone to fling,
and juggles with a nifty flick
beneath his leg, as if to prove
insouciance, then aims with love
straight for the glass but hits the brick.

MEMORABILIA

Here is the poem of the feather,
wafted from heaven or from hell,
that Browning, pensive in the heather,
encountered, and remembered Shelley,
and Watkins, bending to the shore
of Wales, discovered, caked with sand.
Please speak it for us in the solemn manner:
high-flown and slow, oracular.
We listeners have lit a fire
and wait on hard seats in the glow
to pay attention when you raise your hand
for silence, and remind us how
when glory vanished altogether
the sky split open and the feather fell.

THE PARTING

The out-by in the corner of our worst,
most useless pasture has his look.
It is so steep the stones fall loose
beneath your boots and keep on falling.
He couldn't do a hand's turn without groaning,
and now he's in the newspaper for quoting
in books about the working folk.
See how his letters gather dust
as time goes on, behind the clock, unopened.
The track up there has worn deep, like the parting
he dug into his hair with soap
for lack of Brylcreem, on that sunny morning
he took our money from the cocoa-tin
and left before his conscience woke.

FANCY DRESS

The man who came got up as Mr Darwin
explains how species endlessly divide
and seek through adaptation to ensure,
as best they can, the business of survival.
Meanwhile, guests hoot to see the carpet slide
beneath our ancestor, the late arrival,
who rented a gorilla suit,
the mask of which drops to reveal
a small head, like a worried grapefruit
between huge shoulders, and a silly grin.
Our hostess, la Marquise de Pompadour,
embarrassed in her crinoline,
deletes him from her book of evolution
and exits to adjust her chevelure.

SEA FEVER

Why not come out again and kick my head
till it resumes identity
as half a lobster pot? Unwrap my skin
of polythene from driftwood, weeds and stones?
You'll find my fingers have acquired extensions
that comb the pleats of sea and gather
the stuff I need to build another body,
this time for you, my twin, my lover,
of buoyant and appalling beauty.
Your darkening footprints on the wet sand shrink
to dimples and your hotel bed
feels the tide shift and begins to sink
while I am downstairs at the desk already,
insistent, and the worse for drink.

DRAWING FIRE

It's after midnight, and a damp wind kisses
the battlefield as time and hope
run out along the salient.
A sentry shivers in his cape,
lost in a sound-fog: stifled talk,
a tin cup clinking, then a shriek
out from a barbed entanglement,
some bastard pissing, and a squeak
as something drags a helping of corruption
across a shell-hole's greasy lip.
The boy will chance a shot and won't escape
to get tight at the Armistice
and meet his girl, and queue for work,
or live to say he'd missed the better option.

THE ARCHAEOLOGIST

You told me Nero in a lion's mane
stalks the damp woods, clawed and fanged,
to find us and bite off our thumbs
here in this caravan, sagged on its blocks,
the door cracked open like a dirty pod.
But will he find out in which pocket
you hid his brooch with Mithras and the ox,
his emerald engraved with Hercules?
Surface water, rich with sheep dung,
stalls the ambulance down in the lane.
You were my emperor. I was your god.
Before it's time to parley with the police,
I'll make you decent in your poacher's jacket
and prop you in the wardrobe as if hanged.

THE TOURIST

The tourist at this moment will not stir
but stares beyond the cypresses
towards unmelted snow on sharp sierras
as if his eyes were new again.
A girl is sweeping, hushing an old broom,
and speaks politely but he will not answer.
He finds the scents of myrtle and of jasmine
insufficient, like the dark pinetum
and all the thread-like veins of lichen.
Tell him the colour of the crumbling tower
is not valerian, yet not quite rose.
He has remembered a young dancer.
Above the lizard on the broken column
he sees the trembling of the stars.

THE DOLL

If I go prowling while the moon
shines through the fanlight and the letter-box,
and find what's beastly, propped up in the gloom
beside the hall-stand mirror – placed
so nothing is reflected, even you –
I'll borrow your Victorinox
Swiss Army penknife to resolve the matter,
and kill the thing among the coats and sticks
then chop its yellow curls askew.
And later, when my light stays on
night after night as I grow fatter
and try to feed its canvas face
with doll-food from a doll-sized spoon,
I'll teach it that you told me what to do.

APRÈS-MIDI

On the jetty is a grey collection
of packing-cases, a piano,
a limp flag hanging from a crooked staff,
the navigation office, closed.
This is a good day for the turtle,
the sand-caked boy who finds a starfish,
the tethered cockerel, beneath a tree
fantastical in swags of moss.
Upstream, mud-banks are volatile
and teem with crocodiles. The river's low.
Our progress will not thereby be affected.
Inside the Residence, a dusty echo
returns the laughter of a large pink lady
who wants to take her clothes off and be fiction.

ST GEORGE'S DAY

For centuries the same sun has been sinking
here, where we loiter to invoke
the green, embroidered by long-fingered shadows
of branches coming into leaf, the drumming
and piping over, and the people –
who danced today and work the land in common –
cupping hands into the cool mill-brook
which are our own hands, but with callouses.
Beside the inn door, at a solid table,
a ballad-seller and two dairy-women
sing the language we are thinking.
As Hob the landlord gobs for luck
into their ale, and picks his nose,
new worlds grow outward from the sunlit oak.

BLACK COUNTRY BROWNING

Here's where the forges were, the crucible
where we fought fire and smoke and sin
to cast a fancy from a flower-bell,
or catch a sunset-touch in glass
for chapel windows that began to glow
as far as the antipodes.
We coupled on the warm stone by the furnace,
which brings us down to thee, grown up so well
without our piety or taste in verse.
We burnished hammers with our skin,
but it consoles us that our bishops knew
of chorus-endings from Euripides,
as we sink deeper where the anvils rust
into the centre of the compass-rose.

FOLLY WOOD

All haile the noble Companie,
Students in holy Alchimie,
Whose noble practice doth them teach
To vaile it with a mistie speech.

The Hunting of the Greene Lyon

George Ripley, who died in 1490, was an important
English alchemist. The subtitles of the thirteen
sections of 'Folly Wood' are the names of the Twelve
Gates, or stages in the alchemical process, as set out in
his *Compound of Alchymy*, plus the Recapitulation.
They are of course in a different order.

Fermentation

The night is creeping up behind the day
and all our keys are searching for their locks.
To be misled about the greater good,
and botch the things we're meant to do,
is blameless as the rot between your teeth.
The whisky on your breath would fell an ox.
Come back with me across the muddy fields
to drink another at the *ferme ornée*
and watch the moon rise at my study window,
bewitchingly from Folly Wood.
I'll teach you how to hold it at the zenith
between your thumbs, until it yields
to gentle pressure and stops all the clocks.

Sublimation

Leave us this morning if you wish, but first
spare time to meet our floating harp.
Please make sure that the door is shut,
then call her gently and observe
how groans of vanished poets lift her up,
and birdsong from long-silent beaks
resounds to make her tilt and quiver.
On rainy days, when Malkin is morose,
the harp will sometimes stamp her foot
upon the parquet, and make starlings burst
like soot bombs from the hearth and box
his ears with black arpeggios.

Congelation

To find our whereabouts, look at the palm
of your left hand – the *thenar eminence*,
since we are scientific men – yes, yes,
or Mount of Venus if you wish, and see
an old stone farmhouse with embellishments –
a turret and a little park,
my study window with four branching lancets –
all taking shape beneath the sun
while you and I consult your fate together.
Be patient as the landscape gathers
about you in its own good time and weather.
The temple on the *hypothenar* knoll –
towards the South – my own Mount Cyllene –
pertains to Mercury, Hermes, or Thoth
in all his guises. To the North,
young Goldilocks, the green of thumb,
is Ceres, in the kitchen garden
levelled from the hill behind the house.
See how she skittishly unseats
potatoes for our casserole,
and throws aside her garments as she goes.
The roof, too, is of slabs of stone
between which blown seeds find an anchorage
as you have done, now look again
and pick us out among the terms and statues
that make this terrace quite a pantheon.
You will see further, when you find the courage.
A gleam of water, linking head and heart,
bisects your *palmar excavation* –
we are still scientific men –
through working meadows where a path ascends
along the Line of Destiny
to Folly Wood, the hanging dark
that cloaks the hillside at your fingers' ends.

Exaltation

When I'm despondent, Malkin makes me laugh
by reading with that squawk of his
adjusted to a boyish chime
and funnelled lips, as if to blow
or suck the letters off the page and leave
upon his lap not book but album.
Perhaps his face-parts are becoming stiff.
Tonight, if there are stars they will be fierce
and coat my Gothick bridge with rime,
the path as well, up which he'll go –
cold clockwork hungry for the taste of life –
if I provoke him and then set him off.

Conjunction

She is my keenest sharpener of knives,
and skilful with the apparatus
that traps the essence of the strong night air
which is assisting my rejuvenation.
A man is noble when he strives
to garner wisdom and to master nature
and true philosophers should not take wives.
Of course, propinquity and pulchritude
will not be overlooked, and thus
Miss Goldilocks has learned to please and tease.
When my indulgence prompts ingratitude,
she takes to girlish fits of rustication
and then my fond heart leaps to see her gain
the lawn and fields beyond the pantheon –
those absurd deities of my domain
extending limbs of mossy stone
as if to halt her by gesticulation –
then ford the trout stream on her hands and knees,
as naked as a naiad in the flood,
and climb an oak before my pack arrives
to tree her there till I am understood.

Cibation

This evening we shall make your finger bleed
to tempt those pretty singers from their nests,
that thrive on blood up by the temple,
and only blood, except a little pepper
which I provide to make them sing more purely.
You will enjoy their soothing anapæsts
the more so should our harp, as if she dreamt
their singing, let the darkling breeze
move among her strings and make them tremble
sufficiently to harmonise.
Be careful when they start to feed.
You'll see them take a very dove-like supper
unless the pepper makes them sneeze,
in which case they may change their ways entirely
and every eager beak become a blade.

Separation

The past is something a wise man discards,
but there are episodes to mention.
Since I grew up apart from other boys,
the victims of my first success with words
were lovers on a Davenport tureen.
They lived in gardens quite like mine
but less austere, you understand,
with ruined arches and tall banks of flowers
that leaned towards them on the porcelain
as he inclined, with half-closed eyes,
to doff his hat and kiss her hand
while she would tilt her fan in condescension.
I shrank myself so I could creep unseen
through roses, or behind an urn,
and ridicule the passing of their hours
beneath the glaze, until the joys
they longed for broke, in pale blue shards,
and scattered on the steps down to the lawn.

Multiplication

Correspondences reveal to natures
having the wit to read them, or the luck,
that highest knowledge is armillary
in its unfolding, known and knower
revolving, loop through loop and arc through arc,
about the limbs of God. Oh dear,
that clatter from the scullery –
my hip-bath knocked down from its hook –
means you-know-who is off again
on one more of her mad adventures. Look
how late blue twilight turns the stone
of pavement, balustrade, and pantheon,
to pewter, like your whisky flask,
which as you lift it shows the moon
her dull reflection. Pass it over.
That's better. Now let's stroll the lawn
between the trees – those mute philosophers,
who are like us both seed and sower –
and see how my ancillary
makes zig-zag progress through the park,
a skinny flicker in the dusk
pursued by coiling, tumbling creatures
that breathe in daylight and exhale the dark
and are her mind's corollary.

Projection

Please open my four lancet windows wide
and sit beside me, in the musky air,
facing inward to my room and books
between the pale sky and the bare
three-cornered table by the shadow-flecked
cheval-glass with carved vine leaves on its frame
and birds that, in the firelight, twitch their wings.
Drink up. It's not formaldehyde.
Tomorrow, you and I shall recommence
our studies and have done with logic chopping
or theory without effect,
and seek for knowledge fertile in performance.
Ignore poor Malkin, and the hiccuping
he makes to mock us as we charge our glasses
and all those disapproving looks
from she who tends the hearth for us, unswathed.
Such nothings in the shape of things
are unimportant, though they have their uses.
The night I fetched you here and had you bathed
and put up with your petulance,
you'd more than had your share of whisky supping.
Well done. Chin Chin. I'm glad you came
and took hold of the moon with such assurance.
Things are since then, I trust, a little clearer.
The man you thought you were must be rebuked
in solemn sentences then stand aside
while what you are becoming is invoked
and enters – as your old life passes
before us in the bleary mirror –
as scorching brightness, and each gilt bird sings.

Solution

This morning light lacks strength. No doubt
the copper magus with his staff and cape
upon the weather-vane has turned about
to indicate an unpropitious quarter.
Close watching through the doleful hours
will inculcate contempt for rest
and strengthen your elastic powers.
Our privilege is work, advancing
philosophy towards the dark
of which the edge of brightness is a trap
we shall avoid, now we can trace
the root of tinctures to a dormant spark.
Do not be eager for success. Today,
we may not hope to boil the fire in water.
Try once again to give your thoughts a shape.
Twelve circling cherubim with lettered wings
about their shoulders, might we say,
and Arts and Sciences to sing and clap?
When Goldilocks brings porridge in at last
greet her politely, I suggest,
but turn your eyes from her beguiling body
and let your thoughts continue dancing
the Great Word with their feathered arms unfurled.
The daft girl has a pretty face,
but such allurements, and the scran she brings,
are merely echoes of a world
through which we have already passed.

Calcination

I watched you through binoculars
pick small stones in a daze and grip them hard –
as if in obscure shame for ease
or guilty pleasure in your circumstances –
then toss them into incense smoke
for Hermes, at his temple on the rise.
Well, since such mischief has been done,
we must be bold philosophers
and learn composure from the wise
not lose our heads like womenfolk.
If you were faithful to the ordinances –
correct but not meticulous –
the ritual may yet evoke
an Entity disposed to hurt you less
than these same pebbles, if I squeeze
your hand. Like that! Be on your guard.
Rules have been broken by today's endeavours.
Those stones are shifty as your eyes upon
the table as I rearrange their glances.

Putrefaction

Tell me again about that twilit pause
in which the trees – if trees they were –
with all the thickets of the world implicit,
closed ranks about you, with each trembling twig
alert for answers from the air
that blanched your breath, and numbed your fingers
against the pewter of the whisky flask
and darkened as you took a swig.
Then how abruptly the engulfing road –
as you expanded on your choice
to quit the treadmill for the whirligig –
detached itself from destination,
an attribute of which no trace now lingers.
In that I was myself of course complicit
through true philanthropy, which knows no vice.
Meanwhile, remember why the toad
devours the eagle and the lion –
all but their crowns of leaf-green fire –
then sleeps until his loathsome sores
are jewels on a perfect skin.
I must enable this. Your task
will be to praise him when he wakes,
as we shall, into paradise.
Unlatch your tongue and then rejoice.
They are in each of us, the thin
dissecting cry a baby makes,
the soothing remnant of a deeper voice.

Recapitulation

Today we walk through fire, not air,
and you shall weave a wife or daughter
to leave behind in Folly Wood
as soon as we have done with reaping,
and all our work will be a dream
that once trod on your face, and stumbles
away into a nodding head
of gleanings bound with baler twine.
The space between us is becoming flame
as clouds that harden into lead
intensify the afterglow.
This lough has not been fed by any stream
but by the dripping conifers
where we shall hang your dolly knot –
a noddle like a harp, that trembles
to wind and birdsong – gently tapping
the cross-branch of a pine. You know her name
because you loved her long ago
and would forget her, if you could.
The meadows are incarnadine
about the *ferme ornée*, no trespassers
disturb a prospect that resembles
a palm unclenched – a window shut
on purpose to continue peeping –
as light like gold moves off the cooling water.
The dusk is warm, the stars benign,
and you have nothing to return to there
where what you were is in my keeping.

THE BRASS BAND

'Oh that I had given up the ghost, and no eye had seen me!'
   Job 10: 18

You claimed this view could soothe you with its sermon
of wildness tamed
and turned to English parkland, nearer heaven
than you were, choking with the cough, ashamed
because Jerusalem remained unbuilt
in spite of all you'd done. The nursery clock
would hiccup by your bed again so merrily!
I'd dream you rode a rocking horse full tilt
home down the years, your white unbloodied smock
embroidered freshly in my memory.

You'd find such eloquence to speak of vice
and poverty.
I'd have your sisters read your letters twice
and total up the times, as we took tea,
you'd mention rickets, say, or sewage farms
and then we'd smile together as we'd try
to picture your excursions, primed with prayer,
your tracts and Bibles dragging down your arms,
about those labyrinths where industry
disorders nature and befouls the air.

Be still. Although I hardly see at all,
it hurts my eyes
each time you fidget with the parasol.
The sun to me is that with which you'd rise
each day with ardour for the public good,
a disc obscured by smoke, deprived of rays
by all the furnaces of busy hell.
Sit back and gaze towards the hanging wood
above the temple by the lake, the maze
you used to say you'd solve when you were well.

It's said by men who have the landscape eye
that concave ground
will ever be the source of tranquil beauty,
which same configuration draws forth sound.
Go now, as flower beds invade the lawns
and brass glints from a birdcage made of iron.
The new age has produced, in its confusion,
a kind of orchestra of artisans
who own their instruments and wives in common.
Their music is the fruit of your compassion.

LORD BLAXTER'S APOLOGY

From the draft of an interview with the Hexham Courant, *1978*

Don't go and write me up as a destroyer
of the environment. Wild cats survive –
we think – and ospreys have returned. The salmon

are doing well in all the streams.
We plough back profit to invest
in eco-friendly job-creation schemes.

The locals are an inbred lot, and feckless,
and wait for me, as their employer,
to insert the Timpson and provide the drive.

When I took charge the place was on the skids,
and all they did was hit the sauce and quarrel.
But have a glance at this, my Shrine to Gaia,

a proper grotto lined with spars and corals
arranged in clumps, to coruscate
artistically around our young priestess.

We offer flexi-time until the kids
are off their hands. Admire her necklace
of love-bites as the flames shoot higher –

their private lives are downright feral –
and how the glow accentuates each breast.
I'm keen on opportunities for women.

And, by the way, please don't suggest
this makes me some god-awful old voyeur.
In fact I find these Redesdale girls

remind me of the delicate
sciurus vulgaris, our native squirrel,
skinned for its fur, when they're undressed.

THE COCKATRICE

No smoke is rising from the warm brick chimneys
towards a blue sky without meaning
where emptiness and light compete.
Please put your book down on the grass
and make your face a real sunbather's face.
Now conjure up a cock and hen,
horse-size, and harnessed to a cage of iron
on slow wheels, with an egg in it
alive and massive but as cold as ice.

Your mother won't say who your father was.
So call to her, where she is leaning
against the rail of the verandah
to tease a playful shadow. Call again,
until she turns and shades her eyes
in sudden love and then comes running,
the shadow dancing at her feet,
to greet the hatchling and unbolt the door
and be the first snack that your dream will eat.

THE ACORN

*'I love him, but I cannot like him; and as for taking his arm,
I should as soon think of taking the arm of a tree.'*
    A friend writing about Henry Thoreau

Chainsaws have been slicing trees in half
all day where paths are soft and there are falls
of loose earth from the unsafe banks.

Their yelps disturb the potted fern
beside his window, as autumnal air
becomes more pungent and the breeze

resounds like bad news in the wire
but does not wake the telephone.
The world has put up with his harmlessness

among these pictures, books, and cases
of *objets trouvés* from his lonely strolls
for long enough, and that malaise

that keeps him self-sufficient and well-meaning.
The lambs are restless on the hill, a calf
takes fright in its familiar haining

as gravity weighs down his walls
as if to bed the man in stone. Death wears
a smile cut into bark and knows

how weakly sap flows up his shanks,
and also in which chest of drawers
upstairs, beneath his socks, an acorn grows.

CUPIDS

'L'opinion est comme une patrie.'
  Claire de Duras

The toggle of the blind-cord is tut-tutting
against the window, and a cupid
with baby bow and sheaf of darts
is decomposing in a rosy glow
behind the sundial on the lawn,
his dimpled limbs and flimsy wings a-flutter.

Ideas provide a homeland all our days,
and cupids aren't uncommon in these parts.
Look, there's his brother, framed and glazed
beside the bookcase and above the lid
that keeps the music in the closed piano
in this dark room you left and are forgetting.

THE GREEN CORN

Now we're done and harvested, remember us
grinding the bugbear of the bourgeoisie –
repulsive, squirming, and ridiculous –
beneath our marching boots. The century
caught fire and edged our shadows with a nimbus
that spooked the pale ghost of uncertainty
as new dawns broke, and kerchiefed girls went swinging
their strong limbs to the rhythm of our singing.

We learned in cinemas to love the murder
of cartoon characters, and came to find
that squeamishness is soluble in laughter.
Our revolution was a sleep of mind,
to build the dream that reasserts the order
which progress must impose on humankind.
But soon the dream in turn informed the will
and we found breathing enemies to kill.

How pinkly then our shirts and dirndls shone
as earth soaked up the colours of our banner,
and children carried grief and shattered bone –
the Jew's nose, top hat, and the big cigar –
to tinkling music from a gramophone
in gratitude as trophies to our leader –
moustached and dapper in his dungarees –
while we like green corn rippled round his knees.

RECESSIONAL

There go the victims of the winter weather
on that bleak crown of stubble land,
more thoughtfully disposed by far
than when they used the calendar
to wipe their arses. Hand in hand,
they jigged and twirled through spring together,
dancing the hornpipe of the blood,
and drunk they blundered in a summer wood.

But this is not what they imagined,
that fresh lives gather round them, pressing
closer to be claimed and lived
while who they were is thin stuff, sieved
by careless time from pools of guessing.
Their names are what daft rooks have penned
with flourishes on darkening air
and that exacerbates despair.

Although their progress has become unsteady
against the texture of black fields, the arc
of soundless and advancing ocean,
they're moving forward where a gate stands open
on all the paths they've still to walk
to where they always were, but ready
this time perhaps to find a sign
whenever memory and love combine.

THE THAW

'Botticelli's figures, at first sight, exactly match Alberti's description, right down to the long ear into which Calumny speaks.'
The Guardian *on* The Calumny of Apelles

Cook up some slander in the summer-house
that overhangs the frozen lake
and used to be our paradise
when I was young, and still your worshipper.

Ransack my letters for your recipes,
and let your cronies help you chop and stir.
If ninnies shriek, or brawlers come to blows
around the stove, the last few meek

truth-mongerers won't overhear you there.
The biggest lie of all sleeps deep, moreover,
within the thickness of that shadowed ice
and waits for thaw, when it will wake

to feed upon your calumnies
and you as well, you mischief lover,
among the crack-bursts and long ears of air
then vomit the remains of your mystique.

THE BALLROOM AT BLAXTER HALL

'We might be anywhere but are in one place only.'
Derek Mahon

Here is the home of lost romance,
where gilded chairs are stiffly paired,
each uppermost inverted, legs in air
to tent the dust-sheets, hammocking the dust.

The grand piano, like a catafalque
to house the still form of Despair,
is also sheeted, and attempts a groan.
The fireplace yawns. The afternoon

outside is always almost dusk,
and cocked like an enormous ear
to catch the whisper of a waterfall.
With only cobwebs to support its bulk,

a bagged and massive chandelier –
the wasps' nest of a glass-swarm – hangs prepared
to drop at once if you should call
for wine and roses, or the chance to dance.

THE STITCHERS

'The consequence of poetry is shame.'
  Douglas Dunn

What they're embroidering is us, full pelt
through clutching memory, clump after clump,
until each likeness stumbles, and its rump,
in artful needlework, yields to the grip

of grinning anthropophagi.
We're in a version of the Feast of Guilt,
where consequences eat intention,
chewing fingers, howking out an eye,

then relishing the succulence
of butchered limb and bloody stump.
They'll stitch us into grief until we die,
and yet the teeth that gnaw and rip

at silk or corpse meat are our own.
The only exit is impenitence,
or one small window in the word *goodbye*
through which we would be mad to jump.

THE RESTAURANT

'There are worse things . . .'
  Fleur Adcock

There must be worse things than the *à la carte*
consumed in peace, the mackerel –
perhaps with fennel – and the treacle tart.
And one worse is to dine alone

but choose the restaurant with mirrored walls
reflecting crowds of me like parallel
alignments of the long-unnourished
damned, whose slack jaws replicate

in dismal synchronicity my own.
Another worse thing is that when the waiter –
who also wears my features, from which all
humanity has long since vanished –

appears before me with the bill,
I'll pay for what I dared not eat
for evermore, while paws of bone
scrape up their suppers from my dusty plate.

THE BRIDGE

'Satan finds some mischief still for idle Hands to do.'
Isaac Watts

'Seize pickaxe and hammer!'
F. T. Marinetti

Stand in the light of pressure-flares and marvel
how wide the span, how vast the chasm,
in which colossal blackened piers
quake among the mangled girders

forged in earnest, like the shackles
that crushed our spirits long ago.
The din is pickaxe music, and the throb
piledrivers make – a numbing obbligato –

as dust clouds quiver at each crump and spasm.
Now whistles have been blown, and sheaves
squeal in their blocks. New volunteers
lean back and heave upon the fall of tackles

to lift the wreckage, and reveal
the fate of workers and do-gooders
in this inferno, where one soon perceives
that hard graft and not sloth delights the devil.

HOME IS THE SAILOR

The streets have jetsam underfoot, and haar
thins briefly to reveal a hanging clue
of light that means a door ajar.

A whatnot made of rickety bamboo
leans in the damp scent of the hall. Please rest
your head against it till it tilts askew

then stumble out, in skirts of mist.
A square of dirt where bins are kept
becomes the Garden of the Blessed,

and opalescent gleams have crept
among the postcards in the window,
illuminating schoolgirl script

and *noms de lit*, with posies in the margin,
that spell the news that paradise
docks in the haven of the here and now,

while such as we are spume that flies
from nature's solving and dissolving surge,
which rolls beneath us as we rise

to fall back on the deep and merge
where fog-horns grunt, and ships diverge.

GRETA

The Hon Gertrude Pringle returns to Blaxter Hall, 1939

The factory succeeds the family, and gentry
means nothing now. The day enlarges
dwindling pastures into boulder country

along the thin road lined with mountain ashes
where, as a girl, I dreamed of hovering
above the one-street villages

and tenants in them, who seemed smoothly working
models of themselves. Now Europe is at war
to spoil the fun I had discovering

the gymnast and her furniture
inside my head, between Berlin and Paris,
far from this wilderness of useless moor

to which I'll bring a squad of men and lorries
with steel and glass to build the new aesthetic
and smash my father's pile of worries,

despite the finest plasterwork
in all Northumberland. Here is the bridge,
then more expensive husbandry. An oak

leaps up to greet me by the gothick lodge,
and here come Armstrong and his missus,
who drink, and live on neaps and cabbage,

and will not defamiliarise
their objectives. That kind of *dreck* ignores
the hygiene of the optical, denies

modernity its necessary laws.
More jolting, then manoeuvres to perform,
and – *Scheiße* – I'm backwards in a room outdoors

lit brightly, but by no means warm,
that has a light breeze with a little moan
and monsters, signalling. I think the problem

this epoch faces is its situation
here on this lawn. *Salut.* My name is Greta,
inventor of the ergonomic kitchen,

ambassadress of function and of beauty,
perfectibility, in sisterhood,
of social structures, human spirit,

and purity of race and blood.
Don't drop me. Don't let my hair unravel.
My skirt must not at any time touch mud.

I loathe this damp path between banks of laurel
which tunnelling vermin undermine.
But there's a shimmer on the mossy gravel

like thought becoming crystalline
beside the Seine, the Spree, the Tyne.

THE VENTRILOQUIST AND THE WOODEN GIRL

Although we were the one act in the show
to match the equinoctial gales,
our audience left early in the rain

the better to continue drinking,
and spend the whole night breaking bottles
then beating glass into the willow trees

in order to revive these shrinking days,
encouraged by the scarecrows of the village
who own a copy of *The Golden Bough*.

But we have you, of course, there in the glow
beneath the exit sign. Step up on stage,
and don't be bashful while I teach you how

to pull the string that clicks her lips
into a kiss, and wrap her heels
efficiently behind your shins. She grips

more tightly when her varnished knees
vibrate to distant hammer-taps. Her eyes
reflect your future without blinking.

This is the last chance, as I'm sure you know,
to get the measure of the ullage
your skull contains, and find your brain,

and hear the wooden girl herself explain,
with eructations and resounding glottals,
the quick way to prevent the sun from sinking.

THE WATER OF MILK

In noon heat on the plaid his mother snoozes
while baby's fingers try to hold
pretty bruises
of blue sky shrinking as black clouds unfold.

It is of interest to the ones who keep
a watchful eye on picnickings
when mothers sleep
beside Milk Water and the song it sings.

Princesses in her dream wear gowns of green
and link her arms in sisterhood.
A king and queen
progress before them to a sombre wood.

The plaid has rotted on Milk Water brae,
but baby laughs when thunder booms
and creeps away
to gather armfuls of the lightning-blooms.

WENTLETRAPS

After an unwritten story by Anton Chekhov

Cupboards are locked along the corridor
that stinks of overcoats, a violin
has scraped its notes together in an attic,

and now all's still but for these rigmaroles
about his plan to plant our bodies
like seed potatoes in the soil of Russia

and grow our souls in peace on some estate
he needs my money to afford.
Outside, the drenched back of the storm has bent

to let the moon shine on his furniture
and boxes stacked where gravel meets the lawn.
His wife snores lightly in his aunt's old seat

beneath the icon, and his servants
sleep in the shelter of the gooseberries.
My own view is that soul grows as the brain

is fed by thought, and by chromatic
light but recently observed to wit
the faint flash darting from a marigold

or else from monk's-hood or from indian-pinks
at sunset in a summer of dry weather.
That electricity controls

this process has been made apparent
by Haggern in St Petersburg. I'm bored.
How broad his nose is as he smirks and winks!

In times of strife, it's true, our native mould
becomes the bed for which a brave man looks.
Meanwhile, to have done with this fool's palaver

I'd join the troglodytes who live in holes
like book-lined wentletraps, the cleverest
residing in the deepest, with more books.

THE BATHER

We must be careful with this memory:
the context is already shaking loose
in which we all drift back as if we're sorry.

A younger dog behind the house
rehearses a remembered bark
of ownership to welcome us

together with a fresh gust from the loch
that shifts your papers in the escritoire
and worries leaves along the chestnut walk.

The keyhole of the rosewood drawer
admits light to a corner of the letter
you wrote to tell the world you didn't care.

That gillie in his shirt-sleeves knew no better
than tug his forelock by the path you took
thirty years ago, down to the water.

Let's hang your legend on its hook
beside our coats in your cold kitchen
and drink your whisky in the inglenook.

You weren't a bad girl, on reflection,
and there are worse ways to pretend to die
than leave your nightdress to attract attention,

your towel on a tree to dry,
and live the life of Riley, then goodbye.

A VICTORIAN NOTEBOOK

'I am free! I have burst through my galling chain.
The life of young eagles is mine again!'

Each blank page is hand-ruled and spotted
with ink the green of verdigris
except the last, on which he jotted
propitious themes for poetry
in penmanship of strange and writing beauty.

Below two lines of Mrs Hemans
are hermits, Arab steeds, and bright cuirasses,
tempests in Caledonia's glens,
a pining nymph's disordered tresses,
and brigands of the mountain passes.

His father's clapperclawing gob and fist –
A MURRAIN ON YE FOR AN IDLE FOOL –
are not included on the list,
nor ways to creep home like a snail from school
and shirk the muck-fork and the milking-stool.

How richly bombasine and lace sufflate
the scents of musk and lavender
when parsons' daughters swoop to read a slate
and smile on curlicues and curly hair,
should also have been mentioned there.

Likewise an ending in a quiet lane,
a waggon tilting in its tracks,
a horse hock-deep in hay, a lad in pain
who dies in plain prose as the last spoke cracks
and lays upon his stalwart breast the axle.

LINES COMPOSED ON VISITING THE
THEATRE ROYAL, NEWCASTLE UPON TYNE

The curtain rises on a balcony
where hangs a flag and there are roses
in clumps surrounded by a bloodshot haze.
Their thorns are pressing invitations
extended to our palms and fingers
to reconsider pain. We shall applaud,
for here's where opera occurs. A choir
of rioters is breaking song
for brickbats to smash ears and windows.
The roses do not flinch. At once,
encouraged by the tympani,
carabinieri in thin dancing shoes
hurry to compress the singers'
throats to silence against paving stones.
We still applaud. Two wan princesses
swoon abruptly. When the King
resorts at last to prayer they wake to see
him claim no cushion for the greater ease
of bended knee. Conspirators,
in fetters, enter and endure
to hear themselves condemned to sing
through smoke of Love and Unity,
then perish to the tuck of drum.
The sky turns red above the warehouses.
There's more applause, for the accord
between those soaring baritones –
crash-landing in a net of strings –
is all that Art and Life require.
But it's too late. The palace stands.
The smiling roses in their plywood urns
have sheathed their thorns. Dissent is dumb
and music blocks the ports and passes.

A wounded officer brings joyful news,
though not for us, whose consciences
are slow and spotlit in the line of fire.
We have no future but to commandeer
the taxis and the all-night buses
and go through hell, with bloodstained hands,
to reach the friendly embassies.

SNOW IN NORTHUMBERLAND:
AN EFFUSION

The silence that, for mischief, loves
night screech, fox cry, lonely weeping,
welcomes this cold whisper blowing
residuum, like shallowing
impressions of a nib that moves
to shape a word but leaves the page
a brighter blank, the thought unspelt
that makes the after-image of each pang
of headlights half a mile along
the road to Buteland in the shot white dark
a memory of less and less.

And even less and less will dimple, seeping
to honeycomb, a crust of melt
for Wansbeck, Coquet, and the Aln,
retreating to uncover grass
and blunt, assertive daffodils.
So let the unicorns of blizzard rage
about their business on the Wanney Hills
and write a big word with their icy hooves
that means my garden and returning lawn,
where light and memory can strike a spark
from crocuses like broken glass.